HORRIBLE HISTORIES

HORRIBLE HISTORIES

TERRY DEARY — ILLUSTRATED BY **MIKE PHILLIPS**

LIVERPOOL

READ ALL ABOUT THE NASTY BITS!

While this book is based on real characters and actual historical events, some situations and people are fictional. The 'advertisements' * are entirely fictional and do not relate to any actual service or product and are not intended to imply they or anything similar may exist. No 'advertisement' constitutes an endorsement, guarantee, warranty or recommendation by the publisher and the publisher does not make representations or warranties about any product or service contained or implied to be contained therein.

*Except any advertisements for the publisher's books

Published in the UK by Scholastic, 2024
Scholastic, Bosworth Avenue, Warwick, CV34 6UQ
Scholastic Ireland, 89E Lagan Road, Dublin Industrial Estate, Glasnevin, Dublin, D11 HP5F

SCHOLASTIC and associated logos are trademarks and/or
registered trademarks of Scholastic Inc.

Text © Terry Deary, 2024
Cover illustration © Martin Brown, 2024
Inside illustrations © Mike Philips, 2024

The moral rights of the author and illustrators have been asserted by them.

ISBN 978 0702 33119 0

A CIP catalogue record for this book is available from the British Library.

All rights reserved.
This book is sold subject to the condition that it shall not, by way of trade or otherwise, be lent, hired out or otherwise circulated in any form of binding or cover other than that in which it is published. No part of this publication may be reproduced, stored in a retrieval system, or transmitted in any form or by any other means (electronic, mechanical, photocopying, recording or otherwise) or used to train any artificial intelligence technologies without prior written permission of Scholastic Limited. Subject to EU law Scholastic Limited expressly reserves this work from the text and data mining exception.

Printed in the UK
Paper made from wood grown in sustainable forests and other controlled sources.

10 9 8 7 6 5 4 3

www.scholastic.co.uk

For safety or quality concerns:
UK: www.scholastic.co.uk/productinformation
EU: www.scholastic.ie/productinformation

WHAT'S INSIDE?

FREE: Read the knight-time story of Sir Gawain see pages 34–38

EXCLUSIVE: Learn about the Liverpeople aboard the *Titanic* see pages 91–94

INTRODUCTION p7

THE SAVAGE STONE AGE p9

THE ROTTEN ROMANS p14

THE VICIOUS VIKINGS p18

THE STORMIN' NORMANS p24

THE MEASLY MIDDLE AGES p32

THE TERRIBLE TUDORS p39

THE SLIMY STUARTS p42

THE GORGEOUS GEORGIANS p51

THE VILE VICTORIANS p73

THE EVIL EDWARDIANS p87

THE WOEFUL WARS p100

EPILOGUE p121

INTERESTING INDEX p126

INTRODUCTION

Dear reader, how would you like to live in a muddy pond?

Ah. Let me say this another way. If you are reading this book and you are NOT a frog, how would you like to live in a muddy pond?

Not many frogs read *Horrible Histories* books. They usually like *The Wizard of Oz* where they can follow the yellow brick toad.

Most human readers will have heard of the city of Liverpool ... one of the greatest cities in the world. It stands on the west coast of England.

Not so many readers know that the word Liverpool probably meant 'muddy-pool'. Some history writers say it does NOT mean that.

It is now a great city, but it has a horrible history. Some of the things that went on there were horribly cruel, horribly deadly and horribly funny.

This is a book for humans. Frogs can just hop it.

THE SAVAGE STONE AGE

HUMAN HUNTERS

Humans wandered over Liverpool's beaches 8,000 years ago. How do we know? Because the coast was muddy, and these people left footprints that can still be seen today.

At Formby near Liverpool, you can find footprints turned to stone on an ancient beach. They show…

• A man and a woman walking side by side.
• Animals like deer, wolves, wild boar, bears and dogs.
• Children running. Maybe they were playing or chasing animals for food?

THE CALDER STONES

Five thousand years ago there was once a huge mound of earth. It's now in Calderstones Park in Allerton, Liverpool.

It had been built over the grave of a rich and important leader. A bit like your headteacher.

The mound is known as a 'barrow' ... not the thing with a wheel that gardeners use.

At one end of a long barrow there was usually a 'mortuary house'. That's where the dead body was left to rot till the flesh fell off and the bones were scraped clean before being buried.

It must have been hard work for the villagers to build those huge piles of soil over their leader's body.

There are six stones left at Calderstones Park. They may have marked the sides of the passage that led into the barrow. There were likely more stones when it was built. The Calder Stones were found in the 1800s and some of the others could have been scattered around Liverpool.

Circles, lines, patterns and shapes were carved into the stones about 5,000 years ago. We will never know why they were carved, because the people who did it are dead – and they didn't speak our language anyway.

Under the mound there were clay pots with bits of human bones. It's always nice to be buried with a pot.

LUNT MEADOWS VILLAGE, THORNTON

Wars happen all over the world all the time. You may think they never happened in the Stone Age. But one battleground showed a collection of stone-age skeletons…

- They had all died violently.
- Most of them had their skulls smashed by clubs – some had a hole smashed clean through.
- There were signs of some being hit by flint arrows.
- Almost half of the victims were children and one was over 60 – very old for a stone-ager.
- Seven of the adults were women.

In Lunt Meadows near Liverpool, the Stone Age villagers built huts of wood with straw roofs. The wood has all rotted away, but we can still see where holes were dug for the posts of the buildings.

And the huts are not lined up like a street. They were probably built in a circle, and the remains were found on a raised bit of land. That makes it easier to defend against attack. So even in Stone Age Liverpool humans were afraid of being attacked.

What were they afraid of?

THE ROTTEN ROMANS

Around AD 70 the Roman Army settled in Chester just to the south of Liverpool. They met the Brigantes and Cornovii tribes. The tribes were covered in tattoos like walking pictures.

So, the Britons became 'Picts' … Latin for Picture People.

Quick question…

Apart from tattoos, what did the Britons have that surprised the Romans?

a) Guitars
b) Fish and chips
c) Moustaches

Answer: c) Some Britons – around half of them – had moustaches. Usually the men. The Romans plucked the hair from their faces – or shaved them – and had bald faces.

Did the Romans come to Liverpool? Bits of Roman pottery and coins have been found there, but mostly it's a mystery. Maybe they just crossed the marshy land around the Muddy Pool? The Romans could have crossed it to get to their fort at Chester.

And there is an even bigger mystery. What happened to the marsh?

One idea was that there was an earthquake after the Romans left. It broke down the earth between the Muddy Pool and the sea and let out the water.

And the Muddy Pool became the river Mersey and in 800 years' time that would be VERY important.

THE VICIOUS VIKINGS

The Vikings probably arrived in Liverpool in AD 902. The vicious Vikings had enjoyed smashing the Saxons, stealing treasures from monks and snatching people to sell as slaves.

They did NOT say…

So why WOULD they settle there? Because, after a huge battle, they were driven out of Ireland.

They had rowed round to Ireland back in AD 795 and, as usual, they attacked the people who could not defend themselves: the monks.

They sailed up the river Shannon in the AD 830s to attack the monastery of St. Patrick at Armagh. The monks were slaughtered.

Then they began to set up trading posts along the coast. One of their favourite trades was enslaved people and Dublin was their trade centre. One report about a raid on Dublin said…

Women were experts at weaving and the Vikings needed masses of material to make the sails for their ships. And they were useful to the Vikings as wives, of course.

Then, in AD 902, the Irish Kings of Leinster and Brega joined forces to attack the Dublin Vikings from the north and the south.

The Vikings were smashed. The old chronicle said:

THEY FLED, LEAVING GREAT NUMBERS OF THEIR SHIPS BEHIND THEM. THEY ESCAPED HALF-DEAD ACROSS THE SEA

And across the sea was the place we now call Liverpool. They settled there with their slaves and stolen wives. People fleeing from Ireland to Liverpool was something that happened all through history. The 'half-dead' Vikings were just the first BIG settlement.

The Vikings left their mark on place names such as:

- Crosby, meaning 'village with a cross'.
- Kirkdale, meaning 'a valley with its own church'.
- Tranmere, meaning 'the sandbank of the heron'.
- Derby, meaning 'farm where deer are seen'.
- Thingwall, meaning 'assembly field'.

BREW A STEW

The Vikings left those place names, but they also left the greatest Liverpool word of all – 'scouse'.

If a person from London is a Cockney, and someone from Newcastle is a Geordie, then a person from Liverpool is a 'scouse' person or a 'Scouser'. Why? Ask a Viking.

Scouse is still eaten in Liverpool today.

RECIPE FOR SCOUSE

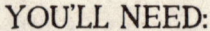

YOU'LL NEED:
Stewing beef or corned beef (because that's what the sailors would use), cut into cubes
Lamb chops can be used, but take out the bones after cooking
Onions, a quarter cabbage and carrots, chopped
Potatoes, in quarters
Water with a stock cube
Any other vegetables you have, like turnip or swede

I HAVEN'T PUT AMOUNTS IN, IT ALL DEPENDS ON WHAT YOU HAVE. USE ABOUT THREE PARTS OF VEGETABLES TO EVERY ONE PART OF MEAT

INSTRUCTIONS:
Put a little vegetable oil in the base of a large saucepan and place on a low heat. Add the onions and fry gently for a few minutes.
Add the cubed meat and brown it all over.
Add the rest of the vegetables and stir.
Add enough water to cover the meat.
Bring to a boil, lower the heat, and cook gently with the lid on for about 2 hours.
As the potatoes cook, some will break up and make the stew thicker.
Serve with crusty bread.

Eat your tasty scouse ... then get ready to go out and pillage a village, marmalize a monk and sell a schoolteacher into enslavement.

THE STORMIN' NORMANS

KILLER KING JOHN

King John was a merciless monarch. He upset everybody with his cruelty. He upset his barons who went to war with him. He upset the Welsh across the river and went to war with them. He upset the monks in their monasteries who said:

The monks wrote the history of the time. Of course they blamed their enemy, King John, for everything bad. Sometimes history writers tell fibs. So don't believe every story you read about John. But we have to award him our first Liverpeople title.

LIVERPEOPLE — KING JOHN

HORRIBLE HISTORY: John is remembered as a cruel king. He was greedy and snatched land from its owners, raised taxes and murdered anyone who stood in his way.

John was worried his nephew, Arthur, would invade England and take his throne. John captured Arthur at Rouen in France. A history writer said that John drank too much wine at dinner. He flew into a rage, grabbed Arthur by the throat and throttled him. He tied a heavy stone to his body, which was dropped into the river Seine.

A Welsh lady, Maud, accused John of murdering Arthur. She was locked in a dungeon with her son with a piece of bacon and left to starve. They were found dead 11 days later. Maud was so hungry, she had eaten her dead son's cheeks.

NOT-SO-HORRIBLE HISTORY: John did ONE good thing in his miserable monarch life. In 1207 he built the little collection of houses on the river Mersey and let them call themselves a 'town'. He gave them a 'charter'. They could hold a market there. And John called the place Liver-pul. Thanks, John.

King John did more than that. He PLANNED the new town himself and made it in the shape of the letter H.

There were just seven streets, and they are still there now ... just not the old houses. John said the people could hold a market. So, farmers and tradespeople brought business (and money) to the seven streets.

So why did you do it, John?

This was part of a long history of links between Liverpool and Ireland.

COOL CASTLE

In 1216 King John fell ill. Some say he ate too many peaches – some say he was poisoned.

John died. Nobody cried. Not even in Liverpool.

Liverpool was England's new port. Of course enemies could attack it. In 1232 the Earl of Derby ruled the area and he thought he needed a castle.

By 1235 Liverpool Castle was completed. It wasn't huge but it was neat.

It lasted just 400 years.

In 1643 England was fighting a civil war – the King and his Cavalier soldiers against Parliament and its Roundhead Armies.

The Roundheads took the city in 1643, but the next year the Royalists took over. It cost the Royalists 1,500 men in one week of fighting and people of Liverpool died too. But they lost all these lives for nothing, as within a few months the Roundheads had recaptured the city.

In 1660 the Royalists ruled Britain again under King Charles II. He was not a fan of Liverpool.

KNOCK DOWN THE CASTLE AND ANYTHING ELSE YOU FANCY

The bricks and stones were used to make other buildings and the ruins became a shelter for the homeless.

In 1714 King George I said…

I WANT IT FLAT AND THAT'S THAT!

You can go to Liverpool and see where Lord Derby's castle used to stand.

Where? In Derby Square, of course.

POTTY PLAYS

At Easter the people of Liverpool would stage a 'mystery play'. The title was *George and the Dragon*. One person saw it acted in the 1800s and reported…

> *The characters were St. George, Slasher, Prince of Paradine, Doctor, King of Egypt, Hector, Fool, Beelzebub, Devil-Doubt and one with the strange name of 'Toss-Pot'.*
>
> *The play started with one of the characters drawing a circle with a wooden sword, and all the action all took place inside that circle. First the actors told us who they were. Then there was a fearsome fight between St. George and Slasher, in which Slasher was wounded. The Doctor then cured Slasher and told him to fight again. This is about all I remember of what I saw as a child.*

'Mystery plays' can still be seen in some towns around Britain. They are very often Bible stories, like Noah's Ark.

THE MEASLY MIDDLE AGES

LITTLE LIVERPOOL

Liverpool had a market and a castle in the 1300s, but for hundreds of years it stayed a small town with around 1,000 people.

In the 1400s it became even poorer. The landowners around the county started to take control of the town.

In 1406 the Stanley family in Liverpool turned their house into a little fortress. They built Stanley Tower on Water Street.

The other big family in Liverpool was the Molyneux family. They were living in Liverpool Castle at the time.

Of course, the two families hated one another.

Servants would fight in the streets.

Five hundred years later Liverpool would be famous for wicked gang wars. But the Stanleys and the Molyneux were the first gangs to go to war.

KNIGHT TIME IN LIVERPOOL

One of Britain's most ancient stories is 'Sir Gawain and the Green Knight'. It was probably written in the Liverpool area because it used old Viking words that aren't found anywhere else. The castle minstrels would tell this exciting tale.

It is a grim and violent story. If you have a little brother or sister that you want to scare, then tell them the tale of Sir Gawain…

In the court of King Arthur, at Camelot palace, on a winter's night came a winter knight. There was a roar of icy air that blew open the great doors. Knights froze with fear and ladies squeaked and squawked and all eyes turned towards the doors. There was the clatter of iron hooves on the stone floor and a green horse stood there. On its back sat a huge knight in green armour.

He raised the front of his helmet. His skin, his long hair and his bushy beard were a ghostly green colour – the giant was dressed in a great fur-lined coat … in one hand he carried a bunch of holly, in the other an enormous axe.

'I am the Green Knight,' he roared.

'I could have told you that,' Lady Freda sniffed. 'And you can shut the door behind you.'

'I challenge the bravest knight to a Christmas game.' The green giant laughed, and his laugh boomed like a bell of doom.

'What game?' King Arthur asked.

'A chopping game. Your bravest knight and I will chop each other's heads off. Who is brave enough to stand against me?'

'I like doing my Christmas chopping but that sounds a bit rough to me.' King Arthur cleared his throat. 'What are the rules, old chap?'

The great green man grinned. 'Your bravest knight can have the first blow. If I survive your blow, I must be allowed to return the blow one year from this day.'

Freda nodded. 'Sounds fair enough to me. Why, even I could win a fight like that.'

Handsome Sir Gawain rose to his handsome feet and spoke in his handsome voice. 'I accept your challenge.'

The floor was cleared and the mighty green knight jumped down to the filthy floor. He knelt among the cracked bones and the dog droppings and handed his axe to Gawain. 'Strike,' he ordered.

Gawain spat on his hands ... well, they were a bit greasy with all that swan fat ... and grasped the great green weapon. The giant knight lowered his green head and pulled his thick green hair away from his great green neck. Gawain gave a cry that would curdle blood – even green blood. 'Aiiiieeee!' In one movement he raised the axe and brought it down with a whoosh like a west wind over water.

'Bullseye!' Freda cried as the great green head fell with

a crunch to the foul floor. Blood spurted out of the naked neck. But Freda soon fell silent when the green-furred body didn't topple.

Slowly the green arms reached out and fumbled over the rushes on the floor. At last, they found the  fallen head, gripped it firmly by the ears and picked it up. The hands placed the head carefully back on the neck and the green lips parted to show grim green teeth.

The giant knight rose and gently took his axe from the trembling (but handsome) hand of Gawain. 'I'll be back,' the man said. He mounted his horse, clattered down the corridor and left as mysteriously as he'd arrived.

Freda chewed her knuckles. 'I knew there'd be a catch.'

The next year, on Christmas Day, the knights gathered in the crowded room.

The door crashed open and the Green Knight sat there on his green horse. 'He never learned to shut that door,' Freda muttered.

The giant spoke in a voice that made the dogs' tails fly between their legs. 'A year and a day has passed,' he roared. 'Step forward, Sir Gawain.'

The young knight was as pale as the giant was green. He stood and bowed his head.

The giant's hands moved quickly, and the axe sped towards Gawain's neck but as it touched it the giant stopped the blade. It made a small nick in the knight's skin, but Gawain wasn't badly hurt. He looked at the green knight curiously. 'That was your one blow. You can't take another.'

'That's right,' the giant said. 'I've decided as you are such a good knight I will spare you. I sent my wife to chat you up, but you were too good to fall for her. That's why I didn't chop you the first time. But you did take her gift of a belt … and it's naughty taking gifts from married women, isn't it?'

'He's right you know,' Freda nodded.

Gawain hung his head and he blushed. 'I was wrong. I'll wear that belt as long as I live to remind me to behave myself.'

'That slice on your neck was your punishment. Now you are free to go.' The green giant laughed and spurred his horse out of the door with a clatter and a rattle of hooves.

'That's a story to tell your grandchildren,' Freda told the happy feasting crowd.

'Sir Gawain and the Green Knight. It's a Christmas night to remember,' said King Arthur.

Freda smiled. 'Actually, it's more than that. It's … two Christmas knights.'

Even after 600 years it's still a good story. Thank you Liverpool tale-tellers.

THE TERRIBLE TUDORS

By the middle of the 1500s the number of people in Liverpool had fallen to around 600.

At least it was still a good place for troops to stop by, climb aboard a ship and sail to Ireland to smash the Irish rebels. One of the rebels was known as Silken Thomas.

Silken Thomas rebelled against King Henry VIII.

Silken Thomas was annoyed by Henry VIII's Archbishop in Dublin, Alen, and told his guards…

What Silken Thomas MEANT was 'Take this fellow away.' His guards thought…

Archbishop Alen was beheaded. Henry VIII was furious and sent an army to arrest Silken Thomas. Then it was Tom's turn to lose his head. But the rebellion did a lot of good for Liverpool.

The English soldiers who were on their way to Ireland spent money in the town, and it began to grow again. The town had a bit of help from nature too. People used to sail to Ireland from the city of Chester across the river Dee.

But the river Dee at Chester started to fill up with mud, and big ships couldn't sail up to the town. So, the Irish trade ships and troop ships went to Liverpool.

In 1593 came a longer war with Ireland, which meant more troops and more money for Liverpool. It ended in 1603.

THE SLIMY STUARTS

By 1600 there were 2,000 people living in Liverpool. One of them was the tallest man who ever lived on Earth ... if you believe the Slimy Stuart historians.

LIVERPEOPLE — JOHN MIDDLETON (1578—1623)

HORRIBLE HISTORY: John was said to be 9 feet 3 inches (or 2.83 metres) tall. The legend says he grew too large for his house, so he had to sleep with his feet out of the window. As well as being tall, he was also very strong. He was given a job as a bodyguard by the Sheriff of Lancashire. But John was not one of those 'gentle giant' sorts. In 1617 he fought against King James I's champion in wrestling. He didn't just win, but broke the man's thumb. He won £20, a huge amount back then.

NOT-SO-HORRIBLE HISTORY: John may have been strong in body, but he was weak in brain. His 'friends' were jealous of that £20. As he walked back home to Hale in Liverpool, they robbed him of it all. That's real friendship, isn't it? He died a poor man.

And you have to feel sorry for the people who lived next door to his little house.

There is a life-sized picture of John in Speke Hall in Liverpool.

DEATH WALKS THE STREETS

In 1626 King Charles I gave the town an even better charter than John's and that helped it to grow again. But there were two problems.

The first was that too many people crammed into Liverpool and made it the perfect place to spread the plague again. It had first arrived in 1349. There were 2,500 people in Liverpool by the 1640s, but there would have been many more if the plague hadn't seen them off in 1558, 1609, 1647 and 1650.

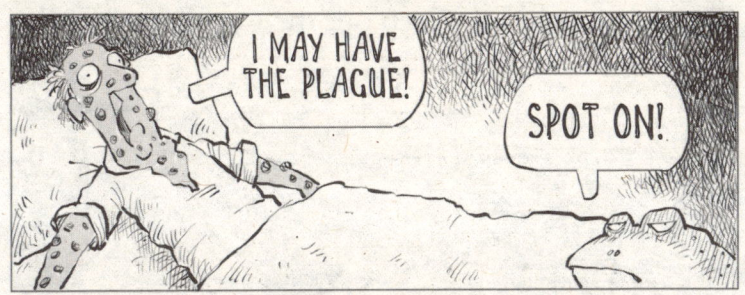

WAR AND MORE WAR

The second problem was war.

The people of England rebelled against King Charles. The English Civil War broke out … the Roundheads from Parliament against the Cavaliers on the King's side. In 1642, Liverpool was in the hands of the Cavaliers.

Then in May 1643 the Roundhead soldiers took the town. They dug ditches and put up earth banks around Liverpool to keep out the Cavalier attacks.

It didn't work.

In June 1644 the King's general, Prince Rupert, arrived in Liverpool with 10,000 men. The English newspapers told an amazing tale which many readers believed...

The LIVERPOOL NEWS

20Th JUNE 1644

PRINCE'S PET POWER

The King's general, Prince Rupert, has arrived at Liverpool to smash the Roundhead rebels. He has 10,000 Cavalier soldiers but also a couple of secret weapons: his pets.

Prince Rupert has brought his pet dog called Boye and his monkey. The Roundheads may scoff, but they don't know that Rupert's pet dog has magical powers. He can sniff out buried treasure and catch bullets shot from a gun in its teeth (the dog, not Rupert).

The monkey is even more amazing. Rupert dresses her in skirts and she rides on Boye's back. She is a shape-shifter – she can change into anything. She can even make herself a Roundhead and enter the enemy camp to spy on them.

Maybe you could see if your local pet shop has monkey or a dog like that?

DID YOU KNOW....?

Boye was a white hunting poodle. It was given to Rupert to stop him being lonely when he was in prison in Germany. It was called Boye but may have been a girl. It soon became known as a dog-witch or the Devil in disguise for its magic powers.

One of its 'powers' was to cock its leg and widdle whenever anyone said the name of Roundhead leader, John Pym.

It enjoyed winning in Liverpool. But when it went across to York the Cavaliers were losing at

Marston Moor. Boye ran onto the battlefield and was shot.

A month earlier, Rupert (and Boye and Monkey) wanted to capture Liverpool Castle and was sure it would be easy-peasy. He said…

But Rupert's army wasn't quite as good as a group of boys – or girls. It was a tough battle. His men surrounded the walls and battered the castle with cannonballs as a siege began. It lasted 16 days.

In the end a traitor helped Rupert. It was one of the lords of Liverpool – Molyneux.

Then the Roundheads inside the castle did a terrible thing. The castle was by the edge of the river. The Roundhead soldiers jumped into ships and sailed away to safety.

The people of Liverpool were left to fight for themselves. They fought bravely and many died. Their ghosts still haunt the area.

In the end Rupert's Cavaliers won. They robbed and burned the town. Rupert stole much of its gold and treasure in the castle – maybe Boye sniffed it out?

That treasure was buried in tunnels under the Everton area of Liverpool, they say, and was never seen again. The tunnels are still there, and some people believe the stolen treasure is still buried somewhere under Everton.

The Cavaliers didn't stay long. Liverpool only remained in Rupert's hands for a few months. In the summer of 1644, the Royalists lost the battle of Marston Moor then lost the whole of the north of England, including Liverpool.

DID YOU KNOW...?

Hundreds of thousands of British people died in the First World War (1914–18) with its terrible trenches and machine guns. More died in the Second World War (1939–45) with its bombing blitzes. But more British people died in the English Civil War than the First and Second World Wars added together. And, even worse, brothers and sisters were killing each other, so were neighbours and friends.

Almost five years after the Siege of Liverpool, the first King Charlie had his head chopped off by the Roundheads and the Civil War was over.

But the battles had done so much damage to the castle that what was left of it had to be pulled down fifty years later. The bricks were used to build the town's first dock. That dock would see even more misery than the Civil War, because in 1699 it saw the arrival of the first enslavers' ship.

THE GORGEOUS GEORGIANS

THE EVIL ENSLAVERS

The Roundheads had won the Civil War and their leader, Oliver Cromwell, ruled the country.

But when he died, the people wanted a king again and Charles I's son, Charles II, took over as monarch.

The small town of Liverpool grew because of its trade with America and the West Indies. Cloth, coal and salt from Lancashire and Cheshire were traded for sugar and tobacco in America.

In 1699 a ship arrived with 220 enslaved African people who were then sent on to Barbados. For the next one hundred years Liverpool was the biggest town in the slave trade.

QUICK QUIZ

The 1700s were a sorry time for slaves. Caught and savagely shipped to foreign shores, they were forced to live a life of peril and punishment. But which of these sad slave stories are true and which are false?

1. African enslaved people were often captured by members of other African tribes and sold to traders.

2. Criminals were never sold to enslavers as they were put to work by their own tribes.

3. An enslaved person was worth a lot of money, so they were well-treated on the voyage.

4. Britain was the smallest enslaving nation in Europe.

5. Many British people believed that keeping an enslaved person was kind and that freeing them would be cruel.

6. One in five enslaved people died in the first four years of life on the plantations.

7. When slavery ended, the plantation owners were given money to make up for their lost workers.

8. After they were freed, some enslaved people on the plantations earned so much money that they bought their plantations.

Answers:
1. True. It wasn't just the slave traders who indulged in cruel kidnapping. One free enslaved person, Olaudah Equiano, told his story:

> The grown-ups of our village used to go off to work in the fields. The children then gathered together to play. But whenever we played we always sent someone up a tree to watch out for slave

> dealers. This was the time when slave dealers rushed into the village, snatched as many children as they could, and carried them off to the coast. There they were sold as slaves.

Imagine that. You go to play in your local park and before you know it a gang has picked you up and sold you. You'd never see your home or your family again. Cruel.

2. False. Criminals were among the first to be thrown to the enslavers.

3. False. Nothing could be further from the truth – they were chained and packed in below deck. Some enslaved people were sent to the ships even though they looked too ill to survive the journey. In 1751 one ship's captain John Newton reported…

> **Thursday 13 June 1751**
>
> This morning we buried a woman at sea – slave number 47. I know not what she died of. She has not been properly alive since she first came on board.

So, when you die you are not even buried with your name – just a number.

4. False. It might have been a small country, but Britain was the biggest slave-trading nation in Europe and by 1740 Liverpool was the most important port. It shipped off more enslaved people than Bristol or London.

5. True. Barmy as it sounds, loads of peculiar people thought the slaves were better off in England than back home in Africa.

6. False. One in five? They should be so lucky. Half the amount of enslaved people died in the first four years.

7. True. But the freed slaves got nothing.

8. False. They were paid so little that there were many rebellions.

THE END OF THE EVIL

After eighty years of the slave trade a lot of people were trying to stop it. And the thing that worked best was a PICTURE from a man called

Thomas Clarkson. He chose to show a Liverpool ship called the *Brookes* and the way it was packed with 454 Africans.

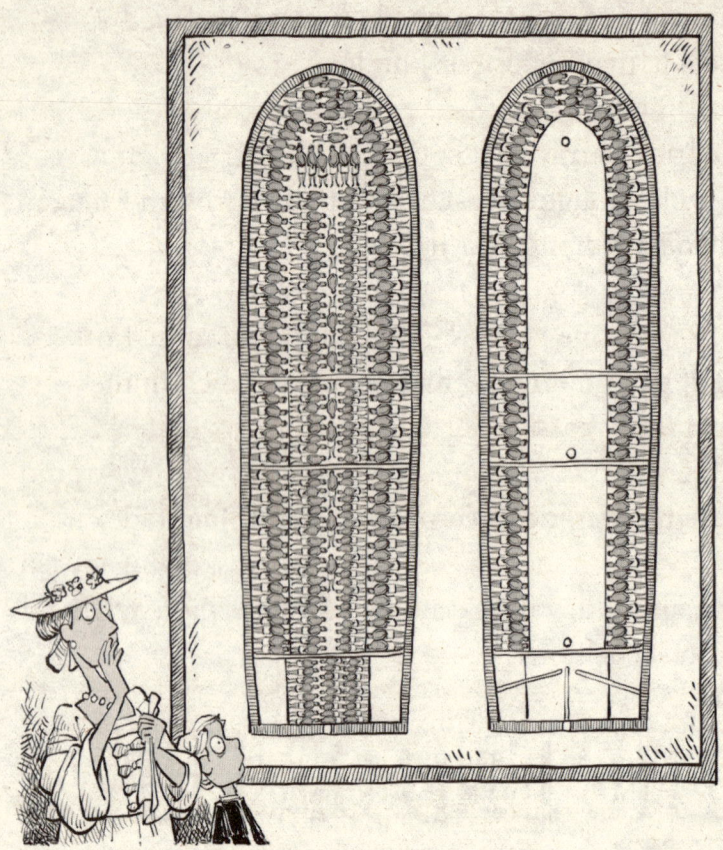

On one trip in 1786 the *Brookes* carried an awful 740 enslaved Africans.

Britons were so shocked by Clarkson's poster, they started to work to stop the trade. Some enslavers in Liverpool would lose a lot of money if the trade stopped. They would do anything to stop Clarkson.

And Clarkson would do anything to stop them. Even visit Liverpool.

What happened when Thomas Clarkson bravely went to Liverpool in 1787?

a) Crowds cheered him.

b) Liverpool council gave a great feast to honour him.

c) He was attacked and nearly killed by a gang of sailors paid to murder him.

Answer: c) Of course. The trade was huge. Not only the enslavers but the shipyards that built special ships for the trade, the rope-makers and food suppliers. The people believed that they would lose their jobs if Liverpool lost the slave trade.

Liverpool soon became the fastest-growing city in the world and fine buildings sprang up. A writer in the 1700s visited Liverpool and said…

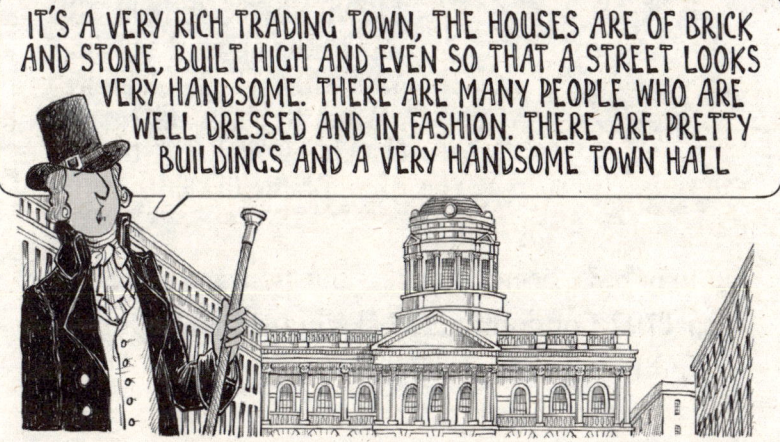

IT'S A VERY RICH TRADING TOWN, THE HOUSES ARE OF BRICK AND STONE, BUILT HIGH AND EVEN SO THAT A STREET LOOKS VERY HANDSOME. THERE ARE MANY PEOPLE WHO ARE WELL DRESSED AND IN FASHION. THERE ARE PRETTY BUILDINGS AND A VERY HANDSOME TOWN HALL

But the writer was not telling the whole story. From 1700 to 1800 the number of people in Liverpool grew to 80,000. The rich lived well. The workers in the docks lived in crowded, filthy, stinking houses with no proper toilets. They were mainly poor people from Ireland and Wales, so no one cared.

The worst houses were the cellar homes. The poorest people lived under buildings. They slept on piles of straw because they could not afford beds.

And those fine houses of the rich were built from slave money. In the 1790s a famous actor visited Liverpool. He was a little drunk and the audience began to boo him on stage.

He stopped acting and shouted at them...

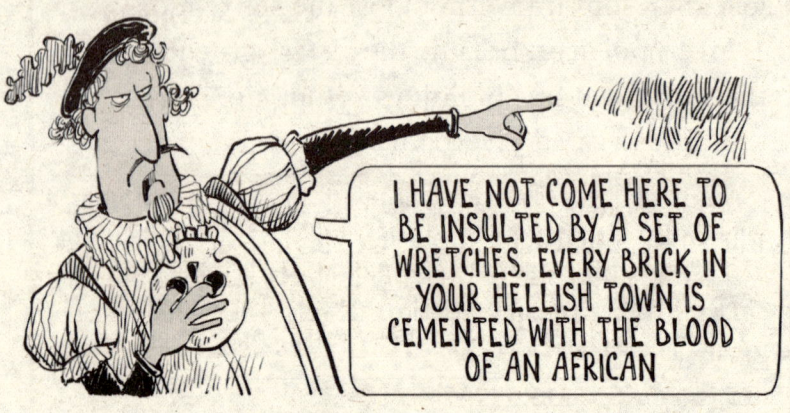

I HAVE NOT COME HERE TO BE INSULTED BY A SET OF WRETCHES. EVERY BRICK IN YOUR HELLISH TOWN IS CEMENTED WITH THE BLOOD OF AN AFRICAN

He may have been drunk ... but he wasn't wrong.

In 1792 London had 22 slaving ships, Bristol had 42 and Liverpool had 131.

LIVERPEOPLE – JAMES PENNY (LIKELY 1741–1799)

HORRIBLE HISTORY: James Penny was an enslaver who made a lot of money from the misery of the business. In 1788 the British Government was thinking about banning the trade. The enslavers got together and chose James Penny to stand up and say how wonderful it is to be a slave. He said...

'If the weather is warm, and there appears the smallest amount of sweat upon their skins, when they come upon deck, there are two men there with cloths to rub them perfectly dry, and another to give them a little drink of fruit juice. They are then given pipes and tobacco. They are amused with musical instruments from their own country. When tired of music and dancing, they then go to play games. The slaves on our ships will sleep better than the gentlemen do on shore.'

NOT-SO-HORRIBLE-HISTORY: The Liverpool group The Beatles wrote a song about Penny Lane, a real street in Liverpool. For many years people thought Penny Lane was named after the enslaver James Penny and wanted the name changed. But no one could prove it had anything to do with the enslaver and now historians say it is NOT named after him.

No one believes James Penny's fairy tale of a good life for enslaved people. The enslaved never did.

In 1807 the Slave Trade Act saw the end of the slave trade in Britain and its empire.

Today the city of Liverpool admits it had a shameful slaving history and opened the International Slavery Museum in 2007 to tell the true, horrible history.

THE ROTTEN RAILWAY

Liverpool's ships carried stuff made in factories to trade in Africa and America. But the city didn't have many factories. They were mostly in Manchester – thirty miles to the east. So, how could you carry the goods from Manchester to the Liverpool docks?

A canal was built, but it was slow. It could freeze in winter and it was easy for thieves to steal from its slow-moving barges. Then in 1825 George Stephenson built a passenger railway from Stockton to Darlington in northeast England.

Liverpool and Manchester's merchants wanted a railway of their own. But it wasn't easy to build – George Stephenson had to take his railway lines across a deep bog, Chat Moss.

But Stephenson filled in the bog and the line went across.

The Liverpool to Manchester line was built in the 1820s. But it started with a disaster.

The Grand Opening: 15 September 1830

The line was finished. The great day arrived.

There were eight locomotives making the first run from Liverpool to Manchester. For the opening procession the Prime Minister, the Duke of Wellington, had a train on one line and the other seven trains would run alongside it. An engineer, Nicholas Wood, said...

> THE EYES OF THE WHOLE SCIENCE WORLD WERE UPON THE GREAT UNDERTAKING

Maybe not ALL eyes? Because in Liverpool Station a cannon was fired as the starting signal. There wasn't a cannonball in it of course, just gunpowder and cotton material. But that was dangerous enough. The burning cotton flew from the barrel, hit a spectator in the face and sent his eyeball rolling down his cheek.

> DID YOU SEE THE OPENING?

> I'VE NO EYE-DEAR!

LIVERPEOPLE – WILLIAM HUSKISSON MP (1770–1830)

HORRIBLE HISTORY: William Huskisson was the Member of Parliament for Liverpool from 1823 and was quite popular in the town. He was also an unlucky sort of man.

As a child he broke his arm getting out of bed.

Just before he married his horse fell on him.

He was flattened by a carriage in London.

He tried to jump over the moat of a Scottish Castle and snapped tendons in his foot.

He limped back to London then he fell off his horse (again), broke his arm (again), before falling out of a carriage and breaking his arm (again-again).

A sore throat never mended and his voice became a rasping hiss.

He headed to France to recover, and did he slip on a frog and break his arm? No. He tripped over a metal cable and gashed his foot.

Oh ... and he suffered periods of gout.

He was invited to the opening of the Liverpool to Manchester Railway in 1830. He was ill from a kidney disease that made him feel like he needed to pee all the time. His doctors told him not to go. He did. Worst luck of all.

THE NOT-SO-HORRIBLE-HISTORY: He climbed on the Liverpool train and set off for Manchester. At least he got halfway there.

At the halfway point the trains stopped for water.

The passengers were asked not to get off. So, what did fifty of them do? They got off. William Huskisson saw the Duke of Wellington and strolled across the line to chat to him.

As they spoke someone cried that the locomotive *Rocket* was speeding down that track. Huskisson panicked. He ran into the path of *Rocket*.

Rocket had no brakes. Huskisson fell and landed between the tracks with his left leg draped across *Rocket*'s line. Huskisson's thigh was crushed. He cried out…

The newspaper headlines the next day were gruesome.

And…

His last words were:

I HAVE MET MY DEATH. GOD FORGIVE ME

We don't know God's reply.

It was not a lucky railway.

DID YOU KNOW…?

After the opening disaster, the first trains ran for the public. The luckiest – or unluckiest – victim of the Liverpool railway has to be Thomas Forsyth.

Tom was hit by the first train to run on the

Liverpool to Manchester service. He had a leg amputated and replaced with a cork one.

He lived almost thirty years more until he was in a railway factory in Manchester when a Russian locomotive blew up. He suffered a deep wound to his forehead. A piece of flying iron had killed him instantly.

Tom Forsyth: if the first train don't kill you, then the second one will.

DEADLY DISEASE

Slavery was now banned but the docks went on growing.

The ships brought wealth – mostly to the wealthy. From 1824 to 1858 more than 10 miles (16 kilometres) of new dock space was opened.

The ships brought jobs for the poor people. They also brought diseases from around the world.

The poor people of Liverpool lived in filth, and filth meant disease. In 1832 the dreaded cholera arrived.

DID YOU KNOW...?

Cholera is caused by a little germ that infects your guts. If the victim didn't get a doctor's help then they usually died.

It got into someone by them drinking water that has other people's poo in it. Or they could catch it by eating food that is washed in the same dirty water. After five days the infected person produces large amounts of poo that has turned watery. They begin to throw up. Then they turn a blue-grey colour. Then they die.

If you catch it now then you can be cured quickly. There were no good cures for the Liverpool people of the 1830s. They lived in parts of Liverpool that had names like 'Little Hell'.

WOTTEN WORKHOUSES

If you were poor and could not get a job then you were not allowed to beg, and the rich would not pay you.

At the end of the Georgian age the government passed 'The Poor Law'.

In one of the world's most famous stories, *Oliver Twist*, a hungry boy pleaded for seconds of his dinner. Charles Dickens wrote…

The evening arrived; the boys took their places. The gruel was served out. The gruel disappeared; the boys whispered each other, and winked at Oliver, and nudged him. He was desperate with hunger, and reckless with misery. He rose from the table; and advancing to the master, basin and spoon in hand, said:

'Please, sir, I want some more.'

Charles Dickens (1812–70),
English author of *Oliver Twist*

The story of *Oliver Twist* made a lot of people see how cruel the workhouse system was.

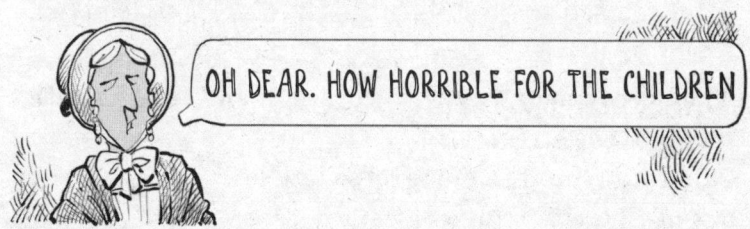

It was horrible for the old people too. Too old to work, they had nowhere to go. But a famous poem called 'It was Christmas Day in the Workhouse' told the story of a starving old woman who was too proud to go to the workhouse to be fed. She cried to her husband…

Then she rose to her feet and trembled, and fell on the rags and moaned,
And, 'Give me a crust, I'm famished … for the love of God,' she groaned.

George R. Sims (1847–1922),
English writer

Her husband ran to the workhouse where the managers were feasting on Christmas dinner.

I rushed from the room like
a madman and flew to the
workhouse gate,
Crying, 'Food for a dying woman!'
And the answer came, 'Too late.'

They refused so he stole bread from a dog to feed her.

They drove me away with curses; then I fought with
a dog in the street,
And tore from the mongrel's clutches,
A crust he was trying to eat.

She died. And the old man blamed the rich people who had no pity.

Yes, there in a land of plenty, lay a loving woman dead.
Cruelly starved and murdered for a loaf of the parish bread.

The poem was meant to be funny. But many Victorians thought it was serious and started to see how cruel the workhouses were.

OH DEAR. HOW HORRIBLE FOR THE OLD PEOPLE

Oliver Twist made people think the poor people in the workhouse got by on a diet of gruel (thin porridge) and water.

Really it was even worse than that.

DID YOU KNOW...?

Poor people in workhouses had to work for their food. They did jobs like crushing bones of horses and dogs to make fertilizer to spread on farm fields.

But the poor were sometimes so hungry that they scrambled for the rotting bones when they were unloaded.

Boys as young as eight worked in pairs to operate the heavy hammers (or 'rammers') to break open the bones.

During the bone-crushing, flying splinters of bone often stabbed the workers in the face or body and the hammers blistered their hands.

To save money, one workhouse keeper forced a poor woman to carry her own baby in its coffin to the cemetery for burial.

Many towns and cities had workhouses for a hundred people or more.

But Liverpool? It had a workhouse that would take how many poor people?

a) 50
b) 500
c) 5,000

Answer: c) Liverpool had so many starving poor people that they needed the largest workhouse in the world.

THE VILE VICTORIANS

LIVERPEOPLE – FLORENCE MAYBRICK (1862–1941)

HORRIBLE HISTORY: Florence was a 19-year-old from America when she met the Liverpool cotton dealer, James Maybrick, on a cruise. James married Florence in 1881. They  were a popular couple who went to all the great dances in Liverpool.

But James always thought he was ill with something or other. He would take medicines all the time. One of them was arsenic. Arsenic is a poison if you take too much of it.

When James died the police said he had died from arsenic poisoning. Florence was blamed and the judge said she should hang. Instead, she was sent to prison for life. But her friends said she did not poison James. The Maybrick's family house was searched and police found arsenic that James had got from a chemist, enough to kill 50 people. Still Florence had to spend 14 miserable years in prison.

She went home to America where she lived in poverty and died in 1941. She never saw her children again.

NOT-SO-HORRIBLE-HISTORY: When James died, his friends read his diary. James had written that

> he was the famous killer, Jack the Ripper.
> Many people believed him.
>
>   Florence's son grew up to be an engineer.
> In 1911 he reached for a glass of water and
> swallowed it in one gulp. It was full of
> cyanide poison and he died quickly.

EIRE WE GO AGAIN

From 1845 to 1849 there was a terrible famine in Ireland. Between 100,000 and 300,000 Irish people fled and the nearest English port was Liverpool. By 1870 there were around half a million people crowded into Liverpool.

That caused a problem. The Irish people were mainly Catholic. The settlers from Wales and Scotland were mainly Protestant. But they all shared the same slum housing. They began to form themselves into gangs and gave themselves names like the Dead Rabbits.

There were riots about religion and gangs stalked

the streets looking to fight. Many people were scared to go outside.

By 1863 there were 115 garrotting cases in London and other cities like Liverpool were starting to copy. Sometimes the garrotter used a cord around the neck.

What did half of these men do when they weren't robbing people in the alleys? They were cab drivers.

The clothes shops of Liverpool started to cash in on the fears of the public with a way to defeat the chokers…

People were not just afraid of strangers. They even thought their own family were out to get them. In 1874 a man was executed for beating his own mother to death, because he thought she was a danger to him.

THE GRIM GANGS

In 1886 the *Liverpool Echo* said…

We are all aware that the population of Liverpool is a peculiar one – very peculiar. There is no poorer population in any large town or city in Great Britain.

Another newspaper said…

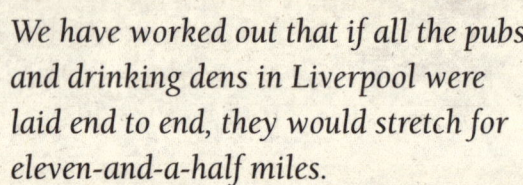

We have worked out that if all the pubs and drinking dens in Liverpool were laid end to end, they would stretch for eleven-and-a-half miles.

And some of those poor people joined criminal gangs to rob their way to money. In 1884 a new gang arrived, the Cornermen.

They were armed with knives and attacked shopkeepers to rob their tills or sailors who had come ashore to spend their wages. Their greatest enemies were other gangs.

DID YOU KNOW...?

In Liverpool in the 1880s, the youngest gang was the Lemon Street Gang. Its deadly enemy was a tough policeman known as 'Pins'. It was said that he once picked up a gang leader by the ankles and swung him around. The flying boy struck the rest of the gang, so they fell over like skittles. 'Pins' boasted...

'I grabs 'em, I pins 'em against the wall and I slaps 'em a bit.'

The Cornermen knew one another by the clothes they wore – a tight-fitting jacket and bell-bottomed trousers held up by a thick leather belt.

Sometimes their robbery turned to murder and the good people of Liverpool were shocked.

LIVERPEOPLE – MICHAEL MCLEAN (1866–84)

HORRIBLE HISTORY: Michael McLean was one of a gang of five who attacked two Spanish sailors in the Liverpool docks. They beat and stabbed one of the sailors to death. The other managed to escape.

The police had lots of witnesses.

WOMAN: Patrick Duggan asked if he could wipe his bloody hands on my apron.

MAN: William Dempsey asked for a brush to take the blood of his trousers.

The five men were arrested. And asked how they got blood on their clothes. When they went to court they kept changing their story.

GANG-MEMBER 1: My nose started to bleed.

GANG-MEMBER 2: We were having a bit of a fun fight.

MICHAEL MCLEAN: The Spanish sailor started it. He attacked us first.

The judge decided the ones to blame were

> Michael McLean and Patrick Duggan. He said they should be executed by hanging.
>
> Duggan was later allowed to go to prison for twenty years instead. Michael McLean died at the end of a rope in Kirkdale Prison. To the end he said he didn't stab the sailor.
>
> Michael McLean was just 18 years old.

Were the gang REALLY guilty of the death of the Spanish sailor?

The police WANTED them to be punished so they cheated a little bit. The police inspector in charge of the case said…

OH DEAR ME. I 'FORGOT' TO REPORT THAT THE SPANISH SAILOR WAS CARRYING A KNIFE … JUST LIKE THE GANG SAID. MAYBE MCLEAN REALLY WAS DEFENDING HIMSELF? OH, WELL. HE'S TOO DEAD TO ARGUE

Some Liverpool people were starting to think that the thing most to blame for the gang crime was the poverty and the slums in which the gangs lived.

I THOUGHT MONEY WOULD GET ME OUT OF THE SLUMS. I BECAME A ROBBER. WOULDN'T YOU?

OLYMPIC CHAMPION

There were not enough jobs for the workers in Liverpool in the reign of Queen Victoria. One man decided that rather than laze around and make trouble there needed to be a way that the workers could stay fit. That man's name was…

LIVERPEOPLE – JOHN HULLEY (1832–75)

HORRIBLE HISTORY: The ancient Greeks invented the Olympic Games. In 1896 the MODERN Olympic Games were created by a Frenchman called Pierre de Coubertin. Everybody knows that. Everybody is wrong.

The Olympics were invented in Liverpool by John Hulley. He thought the cure for the street violence in Liverpool was to give the people a gym where they could exercise, get fit and enjoy themselves.

He was a gymnast and wanted everyone to be as fit as he was. He said…

'There is hardly one of us who is as fit as they ought to be. We are poor, weak, pale, sickly.'

After setting up his gym, he organized the first Grand Olympic Festival in Liverpool, held in June 1862 at the Mount Vernon Parade Ground. It was very popular, so he arranged several more in Liverpool and Llandudno in Wales.

As well as running, jumping and leaping, there were some interesting games, such as 'throwing a cricket ball'. There was also the dangerous 'broadsword' fighting. He brought a new machine to Liverpool too — the bicycle — and set up races.

But John showed that even a fit person like him could not argue when death came to take him. He died in 1875. He was just 42 years old.

NOT-SO-HORRIBLE HISTORY: John's fame did not do him much good. He planned to marry his love, Georgina. On their wedding day Georgina's dad hated the idea so much that he locked the young woman in her room. Her friends had to set her free.

And when John died there was no great funeral for the man who brought the Olympic Games to Liverpool. Hardly a dozen people turned up for his funeral. The funeral priest said, 'It is a heartless world.'

John's gravestone was lost for nearly 150 years. It was found and polished up in 2009.

A nasty newspaper report said of John Hulley...

NEWSPAPER EXTRACT: I believe Hulley was one of the most, if not the most unpopular man in the town. His gym displays were like watching acrobats in a cheap stage show.

Not a nice way to remember the man who brought bikes to Liverpool.

DID YOU KNOW...?

In 1880 Liverpool town became Liverpool city.

FOOTBALL FANATICS

In the age of Queen Victoria the game of football became the most popular sport in Britain. The Liverpool area had several clubs but the biggest were Everton (set up in 1878) and Liverpool (set up in 1892).

Their current football grounds are just 970 metres apart and they are fierce rivals. Of course, they like to put each other down. The funniest Liverpool manager was probably Bill Shankly (1913–81). Shankly said…

I WANT TO BUILD A TEAM THAT'S INVINCIBLE, SO THAT THEY HAVE TO SEND A TEAM FROM MARS TO BEAT US

IF A PLAYER WANTS TO BE GOOD ENOUGH TO PLAY FOR LIVERPOOL, HE HAS TO BE READY TO RUN THROUGH A BRICK WALL FOR ME, THEN COME OUT FIGHTING ON THE OTHER SIDE

SOME PEOPLE BELIEVE FOOTBALL IS A MATTER OF LIFE AND DEATH. I CAN ASSURE YOU IT IS MUCH, MUCH MORE IMPORTANT THAN THAT

ONE YOUNG BOY GOT KILLED AT HIS WORK AND A BUS-LOAD OF 50 PEOPLE CAME TO ANFIELD ONE SUNDAY TO SCATTER HIS ASHES. SO, PEOPLE NOT ONLY SUPPORT LIVERPOOL WHEN THEY'RE ALIVE. THEY SUPPORT THEM WHEN THEY ARE DEAD. THIS IS THE TRUE STORY OF LIVERPOOL. THIS IS POSSIBLY WHY LIVERPOOL ARE SO GREAT

But Shankly saved his cruellest comments for Everton teams…

IF EVERTON WERE PLAYING AT THE BOTTOM OF THE GARDEN, I'D PULL THE CURTAINS

Yet when he retired he moved to a house near Goodison Park, the Everton ground.

When Bill Shankly died he was cremated and his ashes were scattered at Anfield.

EVIL EDWARDIANS

THE DAYS OF DISASTER

In 1901, Queen Victoria died and Liverpool was slowly changing.

It was a new century and the future seemed bright and exciting. For fun there was no radio or television. People often went to halls where they could have a drink and see shows.

The shows often had acts like jugglers, dancers and magicians. Most popular of all were the singers and the rough theatres were known as 'music halls'.

DID YOU KNOW...?

One of Liverpool's first music halls was the Philharmonic Hall, which opened in 1849. It was never a very lucky place. It was supposed to hold 2,100 people but not many turned up for the first night. Why not? The clever, arched roof had no pillars to hold it up. People said...

The roof didn't bring the building down, but a fire in 1933 did. The hall was swiftly rebuilt and opened again in 1939, and the audience numbers grew larger and larger.

Victoria died. The crowds at the many Liverpool music halls enjoyed songs like the one about the new king, Edward VII (1841–1910).

Were the people of Liverpool sad to see Victoria turn up her little toes? Not really. One of the songs sung by Ben Albert said it was party time.

Ben sang about poor people and slum streets like parts of Liverpool. They enjoyed singing along with his song about the death of Queen Vic…

> There's a good time coming soon for the family
> On the day King Edward gets his crown on.
> Parading up and down the Strand, all of us you'll see
> On the day King Edward gets his crown on.
>
> Chorus: Up and down the Strand, up and down the Strand
> Wait until you hear the trumpet sound.
> Shouting hip hurray, all the blooming day
> When our good King Edward's crowned.
>
> Father's going to change his socks and Auntie have a bath
> On the day King Edward gets his crown on.
> With a brick we'll hit the landlord to make the baby laugh
> On the day King Edward gets his crown on.
>
> For a banner hang out father's shirt tied with coloured rag
> We've no gun to fire a royal salute, so we'll bust a paper bag.
> And change the baby's bottle for a windmill or a flag
> On the day King Edward gets his crown on.

No one could predict that just thirteen years after Victoria died, her German grandson Wilhelm would go to war with Britain, and that it would destroy thousands of lives.

But the party stopped two years before that, when two disasters in a month shook the English people.

AN ICE PROBLEM 1

In 1912 Captain Robert Scott decided to lead a team of Britons all the way to the South Pole. It was a race against a Norwegian expedition led by Roald Amundsen. For Scott it all ended in tears…

Scott's team made it to the pole but lost the race and died of the cold and exhaustion on the way back. Some people have said it was because Scott used ponies to pull his sledges – the ponies died and the Brits had to pull their own supplies. Amundsen used trained dogs.

Scott died around 29 March 1912. Two weeks later the people of Liverpool learned of a greater disaster – and more ice screams.

AN ICE PROBLEM 2

The *Titanic* sank. This famous ship was built in Belfast. Its home port was meant to be Liverpool because that's where the owners – the White Star Line – had their offices.

Then they built a new dock in Southampton. It was easier for their London passengers to get to Southampton on the train and board *Titanic* there. So, the great ship never visited Liverpool, the original home port.

Many of the crew came from Liverpool, including…

LIVERPEOPLE – FREDERICK FLEET (1887–1965)

In April 1912 the *Titanic* set sail from Southampton across the Atlantic Ocean. It was the largest ship on Earth at the time.

It carried some of the richest people in the world, as well as hundreds of the poorest – people setting off for a better life in the United States.

The captain, Edward Smith, knew there were dangerous icebergs so what he needed was a lookout. And the lucky looky man was Fred

Fleet from Liverpool. Fleet was paid £5 a month plus an extra 5 shillings (25p) for lookout duty.

The lookouts sat high up on the mast in freezing cold weather. Fred and the other lookouts asked for binoculars. They were not given any.

Night fell. It was calm and moonless. Just before midnight, a huge iceberg loomed. Fred rang a warning bell and called down the famous words...

ICEBERG! RIGHT AHEAD!

It was too late. *Titanic* struck and began to sink and Fred was chosen to man one of the lifeboats. There were not enough boats for all the passengers and crew so over 1,500 people drowned.

Fred Fleet later said...

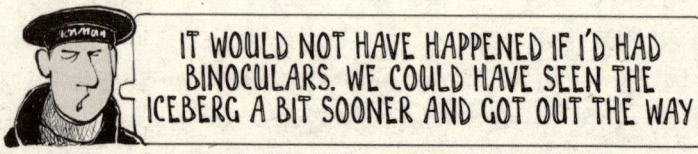

IT WOULD NOT HAVE HAPPENED IF I'D HAD BINOCULARS. WE COULD HAVE SEEN THE ICEBERG A BIT SOONER AND GOT OUT THE WAY

Fred went on to have a long career at sea, fighting in the First World War and then working on land in a boat-repair yard in the Second World War. He'd had a sad childhood as he never knew his father, then his mother left him to be raised in foster homes.

He had a sadder ending. In 1965 his wife died, then her brother threw him out of his home. His life seemed so hopeless that he killed himself.

Fred Fleet was buried in an unmarked grave. In 1993 it was found, and a proper headstone put there to remember him. The man who survived the *Titanic* but could not survive his cruel luck.

One man who did not survive the *Titanic*'s sinking was Fred Fleet's captain…

LIVERPEOPLE – EDWARD SMITH (1850–1912)

Edward Smith was not born in Liverpool but spent 40 years of his life there. He worked for the White Star Line of ships and was given bigger and more expensive ships to sail. Then in 1911 he was made captain of the great ship *Olympic*.

In New York *Olympic* was pulled to the dock by a tugboat and she managed to squash the tug. Oooops. Never mind, Smith sailed her back and managed to collide with a British warship. Double oooops.

To repair *Olympic* the White Star Line builders had to borrow spare parts from *Titanic*, which meant that the great ship was not finished on time.

When *Titanic* was finally launched in 1912 they couldn't put Ed Smith in charge, could they? They did. He was not a lucky captain, but he was about to suffer the worst luck ever.

When the *Titanic* sailed into the ice fields he kept going at full speed. He trusted the lookouts like Fred Fleet to give him plenty of warning.

When *Titanic* began to sink, he helped to stop the passenger panic.

Robert Williams Daniel, a first-class passenger, said:

> CAPTAIN SMITH WAS THE BIGGEST HERO I EVER SAW. HE STOOD ON THE BRIDGE AND SHOUTED THROUGH A MEGAPHONE, TRYING TO MAKE HIMSELF HEARD

Other passengers and crew said Smith was muddled and not much help. Smith was reported to say to the crew that were left...

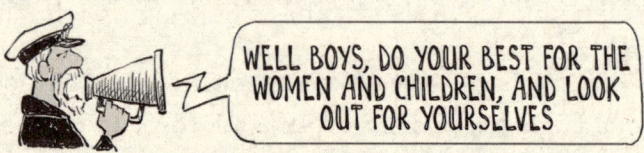

> WELL BOYS, DO YOUR BEST FOR THE WOMEN AND CHILDREN, AND LOOK OUT FOR YOURSELVES

The Captain walked on to the bridge alone. Five minutes later the ship sank, and Captain Smith was never seen again.

Liverpool legend or Liverpool loser? We'll never know for sure.

ROTHSAY REMEMBERED

The *Titanic* didn't sail from Liverpool but other disaster ships DID. Some lessons were learned from the earlier ships but not enough.

The *Rothsay Castle* was one of the first ever steam-driven ships. She was built to sail up and down the river Clyde near Glasgow. She was never meant to go into the rough Irish Sea. But on 17 August 1831 she left Liverpool carrying 150 passengers to North Wales.

The engine was 15 years old and not nearly powerful enough. When the ship took on water the pumps were not working. There wasn't even a bucket to bail her out.

Her captain, Captain Atkinson, was used to sailing ships not steamships. When a storm struck, disaster followed. If TVs had been around then, the news report would have looked something like this…

GOOD EVENING AND HERE IS THE NEWS ON WEDNESDAY AUGUST 17, 1831. REPORTS ARE COMING IN OF A LIVERPOOL STEAMSHIP THAT HAS RUN AGROUND OFF THE NORTH WALES COAST. ONE HUNDRED PEOPLE ARE REPORTED TO HAVE DROWNED INCLUDING THE CAPTAIN. OUR REPORTER IS AT THE SCENE NOW, WAITING TO INTERVIEW THE GHOST OF CAPTAIN ATKINSON…

CAPTAIN, PEOPLE ARE BLAMING YOU FOR THE ACCIDENT. WHAT DO YOU BLAME?

THE SHIP WAS BUILT FOR THE RIVER CLYDE, NOT THE IRISH SEA ON A WILD NIGHT. NOT MY FAULT

WE WERE LATE SETTING OFF BECAUSE A RICH FAMILY WANTED TO LOAD THEIR COACH ON DECK. TOOK A LONG TIME. NOT MY FAULT

THEN YOU SET OFF EVEN THOUGH YOU KNEW THE TIDE WOULD BE LOW AND YOU'D HIT SANDBANKS AT THE OTHER END?

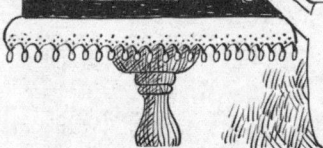

Captain Atkinson was swept overboard along with a hundred passengers. There was just one lifeboat that had a hole in the bottom and no oars. It was launched but was swiftly swept away by the storm.

When the storm struck there were no flares aboard, no guns, no way of calling for help. There was only the ship's bell to send a signal. Someone began to ring it, but the sound was carried away by the wind.

Twenty-three passengers survived. Many bodies were never found. There were no under-water divers in those days.

Some bodies were washed up 100 miles away.

The angry people of Liverpool said that the *Rothsay Castle* was a leaky old tub that should never have put to sea. It wasn't just the drunken captain who was blamed. A trial was held and decided…

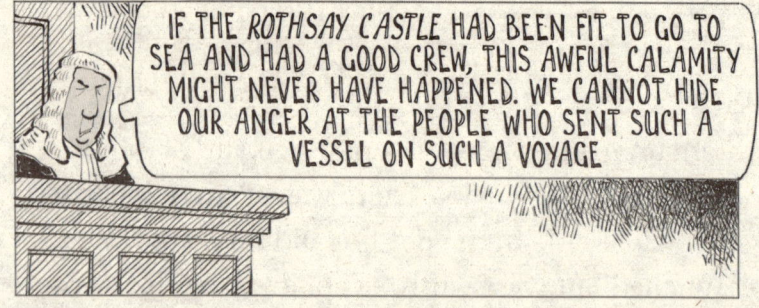

Just like the *Titanic* disaster 80 years later, this was a Liverpool tragedy caused by greedy ship-owners, a stubborn captain who wouldn't stop when it looked dangerous and a lack of lifeboats.

But Liverpool's anger and misery about *Rothsay Castle* changed the world.

DID YOU KNOW...?

Some good came from the *Rothsay Castle* disaster. New laws said that life-jackets, lifeboats and signal flares had to be carried.

The *Rothsay Castle* was almost 28 metres long. The *Titanic* was nearly ten times that size at 269 metres long. But they both ended up going in the same direction. Down.

THE WOEFUL WARS

Britain was part of two horrible wars in the 1900s. These wars were different to the wars in Queen Victoria's day. Now there were flying machines that could drop bombs. You didn't have to be a soldier to be killed in the war. You could just sit at home with a cup of tea and wait to be blown apart.

London was the main target for the bombers. The next biggest bombing raids were on Liverpool.

BOMBED BY BALLOONS

Britain's main enemy in the First and Second World Wars was Germany. In 1914 when the First World War started, Germany had huge gas-filled airships that could travel hundreds of miles to drop bombs on British cities.

WHO'S IN CHARGE OF THE PUNCTURE REPAIR KIT?

On 31 January 1916, nine airships left their bases in Germany. Their commander was Max Dietrich. His report made the raid sound like a great success:

1 February 1916

Last night we carried out a shock raid on the city of Liverpool. Our leading airship was captained by me, Max Dietrich. L21 is 162 metres long and the greatest flying machine Germany has ever seen, captained by the greatest airship commander.

In spite of fog covering the ground below, we reckoned we were over Birkenhead and I ordered my crew to start dropping bombs so they would fall on Liverpool.

We saw many explosions and fires below that must have come from the factories and the docks.

The people of Britain can see that we can bomb them anywhere we please. We shall wipe out their industries. The people will be filled with fear. They will beg their government to make peace. Last night was the greatest night of the war for our Fatherland.

God bless the Kaiser.

Max Dietrich

But Dietrich was wrong. He had become lost in the fog and was a long way south of Liverpool. By the end of February, the German fliers were still boasting about wrecking Liverpool and other cities. They did damage, but it seems they never hit their real targets.

When they thought they were flying over Birkenhead they were 75 miles away over Tipton. Still the bombs killed some innocent people … but spared one woman.

THE WEDNESBURY REPORTER

1 February 1916

Last night our town saw tragedy when German airships came with their bombs. Our reporters heard the story from one victim. Mrs Smith, of 14 King Street, left her house to see what the engine noise from the skies was. As she walked down the street she saw fires and thought there must have been an explosion at the factory. She walked towards the fires, and that was when the bombs began to fall behind her. She turned and hurried home to find her house demolished. All her family had been killed – her husband Joseph, daughter Nellie aged 13 and son Thomas aged 11 were quickly found. The youngest girl, Ina, was just 7 and was found lying dead on the roof of the factory. Her body was discovered this morning.

So, although there were deaths from that raid, Liverpool was spared.

Still, the city was like a magnet for the German air raids.

Liverpool docks did a huge trade in tobacco from America. Germany wanted to destroy the supply of cigarettes that the British troops enjoyed so much.

REVENGE ON THE RAIDERS

A second airship dropped bombs but missed Liverpool too. Airship L19 had engine problems and came down in the North Sea.

The floating wreck was spotted by a British trawler.

By the time the trawler reached port, the L19 had sunk. The crew all died, though some had put messages in bottles and sent them to float.

One of the messages came from the commander of L19, Loewe:

> I am attempting to send a last report. Engine trouble three times repeated. We also had a light headwind on the return journey. This delayed our return and, in the fog, we drifted over Holland. We were received with heavy rifle fire. The ship became heavy, and all three engines failed.
>
> February 2nd, towards 1 p.m. It seems this will be our last hour.
>
> Loewe.

Max Dietrich got home safely but he didn't go on with his terror raids much longer. On 27 November 1916, Dietrich died when his new zeppelin, the L34, was shot down in Tees Bay off the northeast coast.

If Liverpool people thought they were too far away from German raids then they were wrong. But the raids DID have an effect.

Liverpool was a port and many men had sailing skills. More than 12,000 Liverpool men signed up to fight the war at sea. There were men from Liverpool on every single British battleship in the First World War.

When those men went off to war the women had to take over the jobs, especially in making weapons – munitions. The munitions factories had nearly one million women working in them by 1918.

Liverpool men and women served in all the armed forces. More than 13,000 Liverpudlians died in the First World War.

LIVERPEOPLE – WILLIAM PATRICK HITLER (1911–77)

Everyone has heard of the Second World War German leader, Adolf Hitler.

Not so many people have heard of William Patrick Hitler. Adolf had a half-brother, Alois, and Alois had a son, William Patrick. William was born in Liverpool and was Adolf Hitler's nephew.

After the war, William's Irish mother, Bridget, tried to cash in on her link by writing a book. She said...

> ADOLF HITLER LIVED IN AUSTRIA AND DID NOT WANT TO JOIN THE ARMY BEFORE THE FIRST WORLD WAR. HE RAN AWAY TO ENGLAND AND LIVED IN LIVERPOOL IN 1912

Everyone agrees this was a big, fat lie.

In the 1930s William went off to work for Uncle Adolf. He got a job in a bank and later sold cars. He was bored and decided to make his fortune by selling stories of Uncle Adolf's secret life. Blackmail. Adolf ordered...

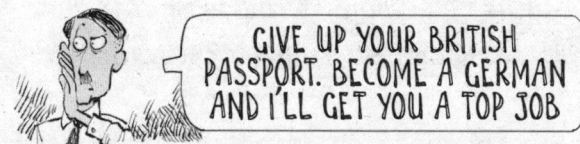

> GIVE UP YOUR BRITISH PASSPORT. BECOME A GERMAN AND I'LL GET YOU A TOP JOB

William was afraid it was a trap. He ran back to England and wrote a book, *Why I Hate My Uncle*.

He suddenly switched sides, went to America and joined the navy to fight AGAINST his uncle.

William's old family home in Liverpool was blown apart by bombs — from Uncle Adolf's air force, of course. Revenge?

William Hitler changed his last name from Hitler to Stuart-Houston. Wouldn't you? He died in New York in 1987.

HITLER HUMOUR

The people of Britain got through the Second World War by laughing to forget the bombs. One comedian from Dingle in Liverpool was Arthur Askey (1900–82). He said...

> *My show* Band Waggon *and other radio shows kept Britain laughing at a time when crying was much easier. I enjoyed doing the broadcasts and shows during those days. I felt I was adding something to the war effort.*

The most famous radio star of the war was the Liverpool funny man, Tommy Handley (1892–1949). Tommy was born in Toxteth Park, Liverpool. British people tuned in to his most famous and funny BBC radio programme called *It's That Man Again* (but everyone called it *ITMA* for short).

The most famous film star of the time was Charlie Chaplin, and he had a moustache just the same as Adolf Hitler's. Tommy performed a poem about it on stage…

WHO IS THAT MAN?

Now we've seen a lot of pictures of
the people in the news,
And we've got to know their faces, you'll agree.
But there's one who's lovely photograph
we've seen for years and years,
And we ask ourselves each time his face we see…

Who is this man who looks like Charlie Chaplin?
What makes him think that he can win a war?
It cannot be the moustache, that only makes us laugh,
And Charlie's done it better … and before.

But don't let us be too hard on poor old Adolf,
His face, it is so funny, it's a crime.
Cartoonists love his make-up, but one
morning we shall wake up,
And find it's Charlie Chaplin all the time!

Arthur Askey went on stage to do story poems and made the audience laugh. One of his most popular poems was about a ship's captain who had lots of accidents that meant he had to hang out his beard to dry. You may not think verses like this are very funny NOW, but this is what Liverpool was laughing at in the Second World War...

His beard was flaming red,
He was born with it he said.
When his mother used to shave him,
he would cry.
So, they let it grow apace,
And, when they washed his face,
They used to hang his whiskers out to dry.

COMEDY HEROES

Liverpool has always been the home of comics. If Liverpool life was tough and poor then the people tried to make it funnier by laughing at misery, just as they had in the Second World War. Some of the comedians grew up in the war, people like...

Ken Dodd (1927–2018)

Ken was born in Knotty Ash. He had to be evacuated from Liverpool for a while when he was 11 because of the bombing during the Second World War.

> MY DAD KNEW I WAS GOING TO BE A COMEDIAN. WHEN I WAS A BABY, HE LOOKED AT ME AND SAID, 'IS THIS A JOKE?'

Robb Wilton (1881–1957)

Robb was born in the Everton area of Liverpool and became famous in the Second World War for his stories about living in the North of England during the wars. Everyone remembered his opening line, 'The day war broke out…'

> THE DAY WAR BROKE OUT, MY MISSUS SAID TO ME, 'IT'S UP TO YOU. YOU'VE GOT TO STOP IT.' I SAID, 'STOP WHAT?' SHE SAID, 'THE WAR.' OOH, SHE'S A FUNNY WOMAN

In his radio show he played the part of a lazy man. One of his jokes was about the wartime blackout…

> MY WIFE SAID, 'YOU'LL HAVE TO GO BACK TO WORK. OOH. SHE'S GOT A CRUEL TONGUE. 'ANYWAY,' I SAID, 'I CAN'T GO BACK TO WORK … I'M A LAMPLIGHTER

Robb was making fun of the Home Guard long before they became a comedy idea in the television series, *Dad's Army* (1968–77).

> 'ERE,' SHE SAID, ONLY THIS MORNING, SHE SAID, 'WHAT ARE YOU HOME GUARD SUPPOSED TO BE GUARDING?'
> I SAID, 'OH, DON'T START ALL THAT, AGAIN ... WE'RE GUARDING THE BRITISH ISLES.'
> I SAID, 'WE'RE GUARDING ALL THE MILLIONS OF MEN, WOMEN AND CHILDREN ... MILLIONS OF THEM ... AND YOU.'
> SHE SAID, 'OH, THEN YOU'RE ON OUR SIDE.'
> I SAID, 'WELL, OF COURSE I'M ON OUR SIDE.'
> 'WELL,' SHE SAID, 'I THINK WE'D BE A DARN SIGHT BETTER OFF IF YOU WERE ON THE OTHER SIDE'

Ted Ray (1905–77)

Ted was born in Wigan but his parents moved to Liverpool when he was a few days old and he grew up there. He played football for Liverpool Reserves.

Ted became a great star on the radio. His jokes seem a little weak these days.

> I HAD TO WALK HOME. IT WAS A COLD NIGHT. IT WAS SO COLD, I SAW A DOG THAT HAD STOPPED TO WIDDLE ON A TREE, AND IT WAS FROZEN TO THE TREE

After a car crash he gave up work and died two years later.

> IF I HAD ANOTHER SIX LIVES I'D WANT TO BE A COMEDIAN IN EVERY ONE OF THEM

George Roper (1934–2003)

George became famous for jokes about Irish workmen in wellies. He said that growing up in Liverpool during the Second World War was hard, especially for the poor. He remembered…

> WE NEVER STARVED BUT SOMETIMES A JAM BUTTY WAS ALL THEY HAD FOR A MEAL

He was known as Gentle George. He made jokes about the laziness of the men who worked in Liverpool docks.

> THERE WAS A DOCKER KICKING A TORTOISE. A POLICEMAN SAID, 'WHAT ARE YOU DOING THAT FOR?' THE DOCKER REPLIED, 'I'M SICK OF IT. IT'S BEEN FOLLOWING ME ABOUT ALL DAY'

Norman Vaughan (1923–2002)

Norman learned a lot from his life as a child growing up in Walton, then Litherland in Liverpool.

He said you should not try to be just one thing in life but lots of things.

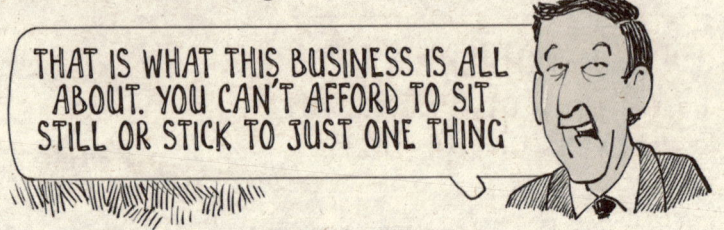

THAT IS WHAT THIS BUSINESS IS ALL ABOUT. YOU CAN'T AFFORD TO SIT STILL OR STICK TO JUST ONE THING

He was a dancer, a singer, a comedian, a pantomime star, the creator of television game shows and an actor.

He also said you should have great dreams but not mind if they don't come true.

DREAM BIG AND DARE TO FAIL

Norman did not have a lot of luck. He once fell into a canal and almost drowned. He died horribly when he was knocked over by a car as he crossed a road.

Stan Boardman (1937–)

Stan was a boy when the air raids on Britain began. Like many children he was evacuated. But his mother decided the enemy was NOT going to bomb Liverpool so she took her family back to the city.

Of course, it was bombed. They were all knocked out when a bomb struck and their shelter fell.

Stan woke up and found his older brother Tommy looking knocked out. But as Stan said later…

 HE NEVER WOKE UP

Tommy was just six years old. It took Stan's family 70 years to find Tommy's grave because he had been buried in a mass grave, as so many people had died that night.

Stan used to make jokes about the war and was famous for his angry line…

THE GERMANS BOMBED OUR CHIP SHOP

Tom O'Connor (1939–2021)

Tom was born in Bootle and started his career as a teacher. But the Liverpool kids were tough to teach. (Not like YOUR school at all.) And THAT'S why he became a comedian. He said…

I WAS A MATHS AND MUSIC TEACHER FOR 14 YEARS. THE ONLY WAY I COULD THINK OF GETTING THROUGH TO THEM WAS TO TELL JOKES. AND THAT'S REALLY HOW THE COMEDY ALL STARTED

Many teachers are jokers.

DOCK DESTROYERS

During the Second World War Liverpool was a target, just as it had been in the First World War. But in the Second War the bombers were better and the bombs bigger.

Around 3,875 people died on Merseyside and more than 10,000 houses were destroyed. Many more people were seriously injured and many more houses were damaged.

The most horrifying attack was on 3 May 1941. The ship SS *Malakand* was in the docks, filled with bullets and 1,000 tonnes of bombs for the troops.

The fire crews struggled as more bombs fell all around them. Fire officer John Lappin was in charge of the firefighters…

One of the people who died was fireman Joseph Gallagher. When the raid started he kissed his wife Delia and his two sons Peter (aged three) and Thomas (aged six) goodbye and dashed out of the front door. It was the last time they saw him.

The shock led to Delia going blind, while the family struggled to live on Joseph's small pension.

DID YOU KNOW...?

Mill Road Maternity Hospital was full of patients when it was hit by a bomb. Two of the war's youngest victims died in the Liverpool raids. Brian Davies and Lawrence Foy were each only one day old.

SHATTERED SHELTER

Bootle, to the north of the city, suffered heavy damage and loss of life. And it wasn't the dock workers and firemen who suffered. It was women and children. A report said...

Liverpool Guardian

TRAGEDY AT BOOTLE

Three hundred enemy aircraft were involved in last night's attack on the Mersey. The bombing was heaviest between 11 pm and midnight when the fire service was called to 105 fires.

It's thought as many as 50,000 fire-bombs and around 400 tonnes of high explosives were dropped on the city.

Last night in Bootle a bomb aimed at the docks missed and struck an air-raid shelter on the corner of Ash Street and Stanley Road.

We are unsure as to how many men, women and children were killed but reports say dozens of bodies were taken from the wreckage. They were placed in a mortuary but before they could be counted the mortuary was destroyed by a bomb.

Ambulance services say that at least 180 corpses were inside.

That's horrible Liverpool history. Bombed to death and then even your dead body was bombed.

LIVERPOOL LAUGHTER

In the middle of the grim horror Liverpool's survivors kept their courage and sense of humour.

- There is a photo of one boy scrawling on a broken wall: 'Beware Hitler: there will come another day'.

- A furniture shop had its windows blown out. Instead of a sign saying, 'Open as usual' the owners wrote, 'More open than usual'.
- A factory called 'Lucky Star Mill', which made horse food was destroyed. One worker joked, 'It didn't live up to its name.'
- The Corn Exchange was ruined in the raid and the traders could not do business inside. Instead, they met and traded on the street outside.
- British Prime Minister Winston Churchill went to the city. He said, 'I see the damage done by the enemy attacks, but I also see the spirit of an unbeaten people.'

EPILOGUE

In 2020 a report said Middlesborough in the northeast had the poorest areas in England.

But Liverpool came second.

As the Liverpool comedian Norman Vaughan said, 'Dream big and dare to fail.' Because even the poorest places can give a start to the greatest people.

One poor place was a basement at 10 Mathew Street. It had once been used as a wine store, then an egg-packing factory and an air-raid shelter during the Second World War.

In January 1957 it opened as a pop-music club called the Cavern Club. One music manager called Brian Epstein said…

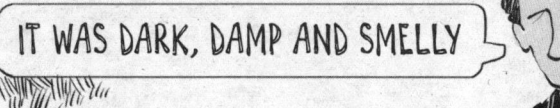

IT WAS DARK, DAMP AND SMELLY

Then on Tuesday evening 21 March 1961 a pop band played there. The cellar was so damp that the cheap electric music speakers were forever blowing a fuse.

There was hardly any fresh air so it grew so stuffy that people in the audience often fainted.

That pop group dreamed big and dared to fail. But they didn't fail. They were called The Beatles and went on to be the world's greatest pop group.

The Liverpool pop groups were tempted to move to London. The Cavern lost its crowds and in 1966 it closed down.

The stage was broken up and sold to fans of The Beatles. The club was pulled down when a new underground railway line was built.

Years after The Beatles became famous across the world the Cavern was rebuilt using a lot of the bricks from the first Cavern Club.

And that is the history of Liverpool … dark, damp and smelly, then knocked down. But the Liverpool people can't be knocked down.

INTERESTING INDEX

Where will you find beheadings, gruel and stolen wives in an index? In a Horrible Histories book, of course!

- airships 101-3, 104-5
- Albert, Ben 89
- Alen, Archbishop of Dublin 40-1
- Amundsen, Roald (polar explorer) 90
- Anfield 85, 86
- arsenic poisoning 74
- Arthur, King 35, 38
- Arthur (nephew of King John) 26
- Askey, Arthur (comedian) 108, 110
- Atkinson, Captain (ship's captain) 96-7

- barrow (grave) 10-11, 12
- battles 12, 19, 47-8, 49
- Beatles 59, 122-3, 124
- beheadings 40-1
- bicycle races 83
- Boardman, Stan (comedian) 114-15
- bombing raids 101, 102, 103, 104, 107, 114-15, 116-20
- bone-crushing 71
- Bootle 118-19
- Boye (Prince Rupert's poodle) 47, 48, 49
- Brigantes tribe 15
- Britons 15
- Brookes (slave ship) 56

- cab drivers 77
- Calder Stones 10-11
- Calderstones Park 10-11
- canal 61
- Cavaliers and Roundheads 29, 45-9, 50, 51
- Cavern Club 121-4
- cellar homes 58
- Chaplin, Charlie (film star) 108-9
- Charles I, King 29, 44, 45, 50
- Charles II, King 29, 52

charter 26, 44
Chat Moss 61
Chester 14, 16, 41
cholera 66-7
Churchill, Winston 120
city status 84
Clarkson, Thomas (campaigner against the slave trade) 56-7
comedians 108-15
Corn Exchange 120
Cornermen gang 78, 79
Cornovii tribe 15
crime 75-81
Cromwell, Oliver 51-2
Crosby 20
cyanide poison 75

Derby 20
Derby Square 29
Dietrich, Max (airship commander) 102-3, 105
diseases 44-5, 66-7
Dodd, Ken (comedian) 111

Edward VII, King 88, 89
Edwardians 87-99
English Civil War 29, 45-9, 50, 51
Epstein, Brian (Beatles' manager) 121
Equiano, Olaudah 53-4
Everton 49, 111
Everton Football Club 85, 86
exercise and fitness 82-3

First World War 49, 90, 92, 101-6
Fleet, Frederick (*Titanic* lookout) 91-3
football 84-6, 112
footprints, ancient 9-10
Formby 10
Forsyth, Thomas (railway casualty) 65-6

Gallagher, Joseph (fireman) 117
gangs 34, 75-6, 78-81
garrotting 76, 77
George and the Dragon (play) 30
George I, King 29
Georgians 51-68
Goodison Park 86
Grand Olympic Festival 83
gruel 68-9, 71

Handley, Tommy (comedian) 108-9
hangings 81
Henry VIII, King 40, 41
Hitler, Adolf 106, 107, 109
Hitler, William Patrick (Adolf Hitler's nephew) 107-8
Home Guard 112
Hulley, John (gymnast) 82-4
Huskisson, William (MP and railway casualty) 63-5
huts, Stone-Age 13

International Slavery Museum 60
Ireland 19-20, 27, 39-41, 75
Irish Sea 95, 96
'It was Christmas Day in the Workhouse' (George R Sims) 69-71
It's That Man Again (BBC radio programme) 108

Jack the Ripper 75
John, King 25-7, 28

Kirkdale 20

Lappin, John (fire officer) 116-17
Lemon Street Gang 79
Liverpool Castle 28-9, 33, 48-9, 50
Liverpool Echo (newspaper) 78

- Liverpool Football Club 85
- Liverpool to Manchester railway 61-2, 63-6
- Liverpool-Irish 75-6
- Lunt Meadows 13

- McLean, Michael (gang member) 80-1
- *Malakand* explosion 116, 117
- Manchester 61
- market 26, 27, 33
- marshland 16
- Marston Moor, Battle of 47-8, 49
- Maybrick, Florence and James (poison scandal) 74-5
- Mersey, River 17, 26
- Middle Ages 32-8
- Middleton, John (tallest man ever) 43-4
- Mill Road Maternity Hospital 118
- monkey (Prince Rupert's pet) 47
- monks 18, 19, 23, 25
- mortuary house 11
- moustaches 15
- Muddy Pool 8, 16, 17
- munitions factories 106
- music halls 87-9
- mystery plays 30-1

- Newton, John (slave ship captain) 54
- Nine Years' War 41
- Normans 24-7

- O'Connor, Tom (comedian) 115
- *Oliver Twist* (Charles Dickens) 68-9, 71
- Olympic Games 82, 83
- *Olympic* (ocean liner) 93

- Penny, James (enslaver) 59-60
- Penny Lane 59-60
- Philharmonic Hall 88
- Picts 15

- 'Pins' (tough policeman) 79
- place names 20
- plague 44-5
- plantations 53
- poison scandal 74-5
- police 79, 81
- Poor Law 68
- poor people 58, 66, 67-72, 78, 81, 89, 113
- port and docks 27, 28, 50, 55, 61, 66, 91, 104, 116-17
- pubs 78
- Pym, John (Roundhead leader) 47

- railways 61-6
- Ray, Ted (comedian) 112-13
- *Rocket* (locomotive) 64
- Romans 14-17
- Roper, George (comedian) 113
- *Rothsay Castle* (steamship) 95-9
- Rupert, Prince 46-7, 48, 49

- Saxons 18
- Scott, Captain Robert (polar explorer) 90
- scouse (stew) 21, 22
- Scouser (someone from Liverpool) 21
- Second World War 49-50, 92, 107-12, 114-15, 116-20
- Shankly, Bill 85-6
- shipping disasters 91-9
- Siege of Liverpool 48-9, 50
- Silken Thomas (Irish rebel) 40-1
- 'Sir Gawain and the Green Knight' (ancient story) 34-8
- skeletons, Stone-Age 12
- Slave Trade Act 60
- slavery and the slave trade 18, 19, 20, 23, 50, 52-7, 58-60
- slaving ships 54, 56, 58
- slums 58, 75, 81, 89

Smith, Edward (*Titanic* captain) 91, 93–4
Speke Hall 44
Stanley and Molyneux family feud 33–4
Stanley Tower 33
starvation 26, 69–70, 72
Stephenson, George (engineer) 61
Stone Age 9–13
Stuarts 42–9, 50, 52

tattoos 15
Thingwall 20
Titanic 91–4, 99
trade 27, 52, 60
    see also slavery and the slave trade
Tranmere 20
treasure, buried 49

Tudors 39–41

Vaughan, Norman (comedian) 113–14, 121
Victoria, Queen 87, 88–9
Victorians 68–84
Vikings 18–21, 34

Wellington, Duke of 62, 64
White Star Line 91, 93
wild animals 10
Wilhelm, Kaiser 90
Wilton, Robb (comedian) 111–12
wives, stolen 19, 20
Wood, Nicholas (engineer) 62
workhouses 68–72

TERRY DEARY

Terry Deary was born at a very early age, so long ago he can't remember. But his mother, who was there at the time, says he was born in Sunderland, northeast England, in 1946 – so it's not true that he writes all *Horrible Histories* from memory. At school he was a horrible child only interested in playing football and giving teachers a hard time. His history lessons were so boring and so badly taught, that he learned to loathe the subject. *Horrible Histories* is his revenge.

MARTIN BROWN

Martin Brown was born in Melbourne, on the proper side of the world. Ever since he can remember he's been drawing. His dad used to bring back huge sheets of paper from work and Martin would fill them with doodles and little figures. Then, quite suddenly, with food and water, he grew up, moved to the UK and found work doing what he's always wanted to do: drawing doodles and little figures.

COLLECT THEM ALL!

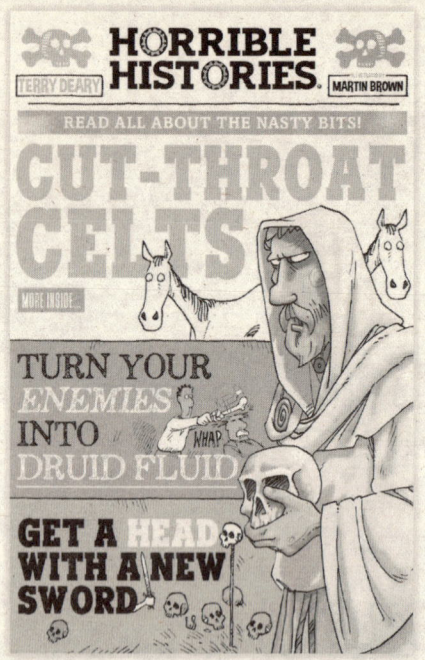

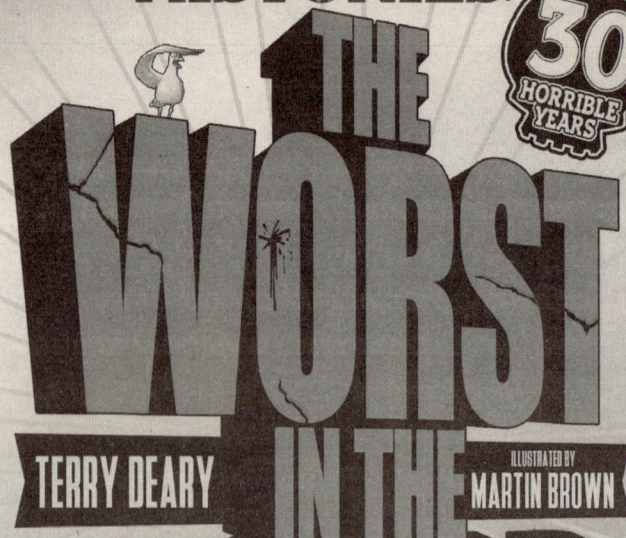